ACCESS ALL AREAS

ROBIN REEVE

Be amazed! Hold the book by the right-
hand edge between your thumb and
forefinger and flick the pages from front
to back for a unique FlikTrik.

First published in Great Britain in 2002 by
Michael O'Mara Books Limited
9 Lion Yard
Tremadoc Road
London SW4 7NQ

A CIP catalogue record for this book is available from the British Library

ISBN 1-85479-145-1

1 3 5 7 9 10 8 6 4 2

Designed and typeset by Design 23
FlikTrix animation devised by www.glensaville.com

www.mombooks.com

Made and printed in Great Britain
by William Clowes, Beccles, Suffolk

**The publisher cannot take responsibility for any accidents that may
occur when attempting the tricks and tips detailed in this book.**

Introduction: BMXin' fer dudes

This little book brings you phat facts about the fantastic biking experience that is BMX. Containing info on its origins in the 1970s, different styles, top tricks, tips on bike maintenance and quality suggestions about building your own

jumps and ramps, *Access All Areas BMX* brings you all the know-how you need to get started if you're a beginner, and to improve your skills if you've tried BMXing already.

Amaze your mates as you do a manual followed by an icepick and get air on a berm. For the hottest information on the best fun to be had on two wheels, *Access All Areas BMX* is hard to beat.

Origins of the BMX bike

BMX – short for bicycle motocross – got popular in the 1970s when the growth of motocross coverage on TV inspired kids to ride around on their Schwinn Chopper-style bikes wearing leather jackets and making engine noises.

Phat facts:

• In 1971 the movie *On Any Sunday* really brought BMX into the limelight. It was a motocross film that began with kids pulling wheelies, performing jumps and racing each other on their Choppers. Bike manufacturers of the time saw the gap in the market and started to produce bikes that they thought would be more suitable. Unfortunately, their first attempts – bikes with fake plastic petrol tanks and mudguards – were not a success, so they had to try again.

• In November 1973, Marvin Church Snr built the first ever BMX bike for his son, Marvin Jnr.

• The National Bicycle Association (NBA) was formed in Florida in 1974 by George E. Esser, and BMX racing kicked off properly as dirt tracks got faster and bigger jumps were created.

• The Yamaha Gold Cup was introduced in 1974, a race that was so popular it was featured in *Sports Illustrated*

magazine. Later that year the first copy of *BMX* magazine was issued, followed by the introduction of the aluminium bike and rigid tubular forks. And the company 'BMX Products Inc.' (later to become 'Mongoose') produced the first aluminium-made motomag wheels.

• The American Bicycle Association (ABA) was founded in 1977 to organize all the races across America under one sanctioning body.

• By the end of 1978 bikes like Mongoose, Redline, Diamond Back and Raleigh were on the market.

• At the end of the 1970s, Bob Haro, an illustrator, took his bike to the skate parks and developed 'freestyle'. He taught his editor's son these new tricks and the editor was so impressed he made them a feature in his magazine *BMX Action.*

• In 1984 *Freestyle* magazine was created, which helped to create BMX's golden years from 1986-1988.

• By the end of the 1980s, the BMX market was so saturated it collapsed under its own weight and went underground, but not before creating the roots of the BMXing that we see in today's revival.

Equipment – the essentials

The Bike

Check out the massive range of BMX rigs available by going to your local bike shop, or surf the Net to find out where the biggest retailer of BMX bikes can be found in your area. It'll be worth the journey just to see how many rigs you'll have to choose from.

Brakes:
BMX rigs usually have cantilever brakes – the ones mounted directly on the front wheel fork and the seat stay.

Frame:
Generally, the lighter the frame, the more expensive the bike. Most BMX frames are made of aluminium and cro-moly (a metal alloy), a medium weight.

Handlebars:
It's better to have low, aerodynamic handlebars to maximize control while

minimizing shock to the wrists.

Saddle:
Comfort is essential. Choose a saddle that'll help you to bear the bumps and thuds while you attempt new tricks.

Suspension systems:
Some bikes – known as 'rigid' –

have no suspension systems, just shock absorbers built into the handlebar stem or seat post. Others have a front suspension system, while the more expensive ones have a full suspension (sometimes known as a 'boing-boing') with shock absorbers built into the seat as well as the handlebars.

Tyres:

BMX tyres are usually wide and knobbly for maximum traction and control. Their thickness helps to act as a shock absorber.

Safety gear:

BMXing is not the safest of sports, so it's better to have a little protection before you attempt any daring tricks.

Helmets:

Also known as 'skid lids', helmets are vital to BMXers. It's worth paying a little extra for these.

Padding:

Wearing knee-pads, shin-pads and elbow-pads may make you feel a little over-protected, but you'll be glad of them if you fall off in the middle of a concrete jump.

Gloves:

Gloves can sometimes give you a better grip than just bare hands. Also, if you do happen to come off your rig unexpectedly, you'll save your hands from possible damage.

The word on the street: an A-Z of BMX

Air – getting the bike off the ground

Bail – to jump off mid-trick to avoid a wipeout

Ballooner – a cruiser

Bars – handlebars

Berm – a bank used to make a turn

Big rig – a cruiser

Bombing – going downhill as fast as you can

Bowgelled – a string of losses or wipeouts

Café racer – a customized bike

Dialled in – fine tuned

Factory fide – full sponsorship

Fakie – do a ride or a trick backwards

Grips – handlebar grips

Gyro – a little mechanical wonder that allows your bars to spin as many times as you want without cable tangling

High side – coming into a corner too hard and flipping off the side of the bike

Hubs – the centre axle of your wheel

Land – pull off a trick successfully

Late – pull off a trick at the very last minute

Locked in – getting into a nice chunky, stable position while grinding

Motion lotion – chain lube, oil, lubrication etc...

Moto – eight racers in the same class

Pegs – metal stubs that stick out either side of the axle for grinds and tricks

Plugs – ends that keep your grip on the bars

Pro – someone who's paid to ride

Qual – nearly the best, very good

Rig – a bike

Rims – the metal frame round the inner wheel

Session (jam) – going for a ride with your friends

Scuffing – using your foot to move the bike backwards or forwards by pushing it against the tyre

Sketchy – a slightly dodgy trick

Sprocket – the big cog that connects to the pedals and drives the chain

Stoked – happy and up for it

Swoop – to pass someone on a turn

Tombstone – to pull a move that wipes out another rider

Tricked up – a bike that has all the best parts

Under the gun – under a lot of competition pressure

Wipeout – a fall

BMX Riding Styles

Street

Street riding is one of the rawest forms of BMX riding. Street is basically hitting a town or city and riding around looking for obstacles that you can use, e.g. benches, steps, rails and kerbs. Riders work out routes that can follow challenging lines through a town's naturally occurring courses. Street comps are park set-ups made to imitate good rides you might find in the city, containing courses of ramps, rails and fun boxes placed closely together to create smooth and technical runs.

Vert

Vert is one of the most difficult forms of BMX riding. Vert is basically a ramp that looks like a pipe cut in half, with sides varying from about 6 to 12 feet high. Riding the ramp is difficult enough but then you have to get air off the lip of the ramp in

order to pull off different technical tricks. Some riders can pull sick tricks at up to 15 feet clear of the lip. Virtually all riders wear some sort of padding or protective gear, as falling from 15 feet in the air and landing wrapped round a metal frame isn't so great...

Flatland

Flatland is the really technical area of BMXing. Riders use specially designed flatland bikes that have gyros, full pegs, short frames and are really lightweight. Flatland is performed on smooth, flat surfaces – car parks are ideal – and riders pull off insanely technical tricks like gyrating, scuffing and spinning in tight circles. Flatland takes a huge amount of practice but it's one of the least painful riding styles and everyone appreciates a good flatlander.

Dirt jumping

Dirt jumping is one of the most popular
forms of riding, especially when you can
get huge airs off homemade dirt jumps
(see section on dirt-jump building – p.82).
Riders hit jumps up to 6 feet high with up
to 25 feet gaps. Most dirt jumps look like
two mounds of earth with a gap in the
middle. You ride up one side, clear the
gap and land riding down the other
mound.

The art to dirt jumping is big fat tricks
whilst making as much air as possible.
Most dirt bikes are lightweight, very
tough (48 spokes, three-piece cranked,
tube welded) and riders tend to ride with

a slick tyre on the back and a mud tyre on the front for the best combo of speed and grip.

Racing

Racing is the oldest form of BMXing and came about from kids in the 1970s trying to

copy their motorcycle heroes. Back in those days tracks were a much rougher terrain with more jumps and obstacles. Today's tracks are faster and smoother with sets of double and triple jumps. The bikes are lightweight 20-inchers with titanium or aluminium frames.

Trix and tips

Street & flatland

Manual

Roll along the
ground slowly,
positioning the
ball of your
strongest foot
towards the back
of the pedal. Pull
up on your bars
and push down on
your dominant
pedal. Use both
pedals to move

the bike forwards on the back wheel, then keep the front wheel up while coasting. You can also do this on the rear pegs as well – simply pull up your bars and coast.

Wheelie

A pedalling manual. After pulling up your bars and suspending the front wheel in mid-air, make sure your weight stays over the back tyre and keep on pedalling for as long as possible.

Bunny hop

This basically involves making the bike 'jump'. Lean back over the seat and pull the bars up into a wheelie, then immediately jump upwards, putting a little pressure downwards on the bars, and tense your feet against the pedals to help pull up the back of the bike (not too much or you will nose-dive). This will bring the back wheel off the ground, making a successful bunny hop, which can be repeated over and over again.

Following each step carefully should help you complete the trick in a smooth, fluid motion.

Icepick

This is when you bunny hop on to an obstacle, but only land on one of the rear pegs. Balance as long as you can and then bunny hop off. The trick is to keep your weight at the back of the bike over the peg, as this will help you hop back off it.

Nosepick

Go up to any kerb or obstacle, bunny hop on to it, but land only on your front wheel. You have to land with the front brake on and keep your weight over the bars. This is a good starting point for lots of variations.

Toothpick
This is the same as a nosepick, but stall on the front peg instead of the front wheel. Keep your weight over the front of the bike and hold until you bunny hop back off again.

37

Double peg grind

Ride up to any kerb or grindable surface at a gentle angle and bunny hop so both left-hand or right-hand pegs land on the kerb at the same time. Keep your weight over the pegs and grind across the surface for as long as you can. When you want to pull off, lift the front wheel first and tilt it off the kerb, and the rest will follow.

Feeble grind

Ride alongside the kerb and bunny hop, but land with only your back peg on the kerb and your front wheel touching the ground. Grind like this for a while then steer away to pull off.

Smith grind

Hop on to a kerb and land with your back wheel on the kerb and your front peg on the edge of the kerb so it can grind. This is quite hard to balance at first, but try to keep your weight on the kerbside of the bike to avoid tipping off the kerb.

Icepick grind

This trick takes a lot of balance and is hard to hold for a long time. Hop up on to a kerb and land so you grind only on the back peg. Keep your weight over the back of the bike, leaning kerbside. Try to keep the bike as straight as possible to avoid pinching the kerb with your back tyre and stalling.

Nosepick grind

This one's pretty difficult. Hop up next to the edge of the kerb and push down on your bars so that you land on your front peg only. Keep your weight down on the bars but also lean back at the same time. To release, take the pressure off the bars

and pull up
leaning back hard
at the same time,
hopping off the
kerb.

Endo
Start by riding
slowly. Put your
right foot in the
gap between
your forks and
on top of the
tyre to brake the
bike. At the same
time, shift your
weight on to the

bars and stop the wheel with your foot. The back end will lift up in the air. Hold the position using your left foot to stop the frame moving out of control. If using your foot to brake seems too difficult you can apply the front brake hard instead. Be careful because it's very easy to go over the bars.

Bar hop

Get up a gentle speed and start to coast. Stand up on the pedals and jump. Bend your knees and use your arms to help pull your legs up under you, so can get your feet over the bars. Land sitting on the bars with your feet on your front pegs. To keep forward motion, use one of your feet to kick the front wheel forwards along the tyre. This trick involves a lot of balance so it's better to practise first by jumping over the bars and landing clear of the bike on your feet. You can also practise how to balance yourself when sitting on the bars, and try coasting using your left hand to grip the seat.

Pogo

Stand on your rear pegs and coast at a slow speed. Now pull a little Endo using your front brake (you only need a few inches). As the back of the bike comes back down, grip the rear brake just before the tyre hits the ground and lean back hard. Use your arms to pull the bars up so you are in a manual position. Hold the balance and now simply hop up and down on the back wheel.

Turner

Do an Endo, but put your weight to one side of the bike and spin with the bike 180° on the front wheel.

Rockwalk

Ride in a small circle. Engage the front brake, lift the back of your bike up and spin around the back end 180⁰. After the back wheel comes down, use your momentum to lift up the front end and spin another 180⁰ on the back wheel.

Keep going as many times as you can. Eventually you'll be able to do this without brakes.

Tailwhip

Put your left foot on the front left peg, then squeeze the front brake so that your back wheel is about 2 inches off the ground. Tilt your weight a tiny bit to the right to start the frame spinning, and at the same time, lift your right foot over the frame and put it on the back of the front tyre. As the frame spins to about 120°, release the front brake for a fraction of a second and wheel your front tyre back a tiny bit with your foot, to speed up the spin. When the frame comes back

360^0 step over with your left foot back on the peg, and stop the frame spinning by putting your right foot on the top tube. Drop the back end down and reposition yourself back on the pedals. It's not easy, but keep trying.

Squeaker

Ride a slow pace, put your left foot on the front left peg and do a small Endo using the front brake. Keep your right foot on the right pedal to stabilize the frame, keeping your balance, and wheel the bike backwards using your right foot to scuff the front tyre backwards, a little movement at a time. You'll have to release your brake a fraction of a second every time you wheel a little bit backwards.

Funky chicken

Put your left foot on the left front peg and pull an Endo. At the same time, grab the seat with your left hand and

lift your right
leg over the
bars so that
your right foot
touches the
front tyre and
roll around in
circles. Every
time you scuff
the front, tyre
forwards you
must release
the front brake.

Fire hydrant

First, you need to be able to coast the bike with your left foot on the front left peg and your right foot on the back left peg. Now, without touching the brakes, take your right foot off and push the ground with it once. This will make you spin on both the front pegs, about 180° or more, so you are facing backwards. Next, put a little pressure on the bars so that the back wheel lifts off the ground. Hit the front brakes hard, and then the tail will swing round and meet you like a tailwhip. Jump on the bike and ride away.

Trix and tips
- dirt

One-hander, no-hander

While making air, take one of your hands off the bars and put it back on again before you land. A no-hander is the same, but you take both hands off the bars.

One-footer, no-footer

Like the one-hander, take one foot off while making air. For the no-footer, take both feet off. Remember, with the no-footer make sure you get your feet back on the pedals before you land...

Nothing

Learn the no-footers and no-handers first. The 'nothing' is the next phase. While in the air, let go with both hands and take both feet off the pedals. It's easier to grab the bars again first to help you re-position your feet on the pedals.

X-up

While in the air, turn your bars 180° so your arms are crossed over, and then turn them back before you land.

Wheelie turn down

Like an x-up, but do the x-up when the bike is in a wheelie position in the air.

One-foot land
Simply land with only one foot on the pedals.

One-hander lander
Like the one-foot land: land gripping the bars with only one hand.

Tabletop
Get big air off your jump and tilt the bike so that it is horizontal in the air. Bring the bike level again and land.

One-foot tabletop
While doing your tabletop, take the foot off the pedal that is facing towards the ground. As you level out the bike your

foot will fall back into position on the pedal.

Kick out

It's a bit like a motocross tailwhip. Get a good air and flick the back end of the bike out between 45° and 90°. Pull it back straight and land it.

Sit down

This is a good trick to help you get that extra height clearance. When you reach the peak of your jump, pull your bike up underneath you so you're in the sitting position. Then land, still in the sitting position.

One-foot x-up

While doing your x-up, kick your leg backwards off the pedals at about 45°. Hold it for as long as you can and then straighten_out to land.

Bar spin

This trick requires a good amount of air time. Grip your bike with your knees and use your right hand to pull the handlebars back sharply, while letting go of the left grip simultaneously. This will spin the bars. Let the bars do a 360° (or more) and then catch them before landing.

Suicide no-hander

This is just a slightly cooler no-hander. Make air and grip the bike with your legs, then let go with both hands. Then stretch your arms out to the side so you are making a cross position. The longer you hold it, and the further back you pull your arms, the better the trick.

Suicide barspin

This time, while your bars are spinning, put your arms in the suicide no-hander position.

Can-can

Firstly, get air, then choose a leg and throw it over the top tube so you are riding side-saddle. Then simply put it back on the pedal again and land.

No-foot can-can
This time, take one foot off the pedal and throw the other leg over, so both legs are on the same side but neither are on the pedals.

Kamikaze

This trick needs big air. Hit your jump hard and while you're in the air let go of the grips and lean over the bars. Use your chest to keep the bars straight and then stretch out your arms either side, a bit like a suicide no-hander. Grab the bars again to help pull yourself upright.

Disco

Put your left arm up in the air, make a fist and kick your right leg out and back. (*Saturday Night Fever* pose)

Seat-grab x-up

As you leave the lip of the ramp, reach back with your left hand, grab the seat and, at the same time, use your right hand to pull the bars 180° (x-up). Lean back as much as you can. Use your left hand to push off the seat to help straighten you up to land.

Double-seat grab

Get up a good air. Lean back off the seat and grab it with

both hands. Be careful when letting go of the bars not to knock them into a spin or this will make it harder to grab them again when coming in to land. The further you can lean your body back away from the seat the better.

Kickout barspin
Kick out the bike to about 90°. With both hands, bring your bars round 90° so they line up with the top tube. Then, with one swift throw, spin them the rest of the way round (a complete barspin). Remember to grip the bike with your legs while spinning. Once you have caught the bars again, bring the bike level and land it.

Superman

This is where things start to get a little tricky. Firstly you need big air. As you're coming up to the peak of your jump, take both feet off the pedals and let your legs hang out behind you (yes, you look like Superman).

Remember to grip those bars tight and pull yourself back on to the pedals before you land.

Superman seat-grab
While doing the Superman, let go with your weakest hand and grab the seat.

Front flip
Ride at your jump really fast. As you reach the lip of the jump, hit your front brake hard and throw your bodyweight upwards and forwards over the bars. This trick will stop you making as much distance at first, so use jumps with smaller gaps. The best way to land at first is manual (back wheel) because it's the least painful.

Backflip

Make sure you use a jump with a nice popping kick. You need to be leaning far back even before you leave the ground. Throw your bodyweight backwards and somersault. Try to land on the back wheels as front wheel dives aren't too pretty.

Candy bar

Take your favourite foot off the pedal and pass it through your arms, resting it on the handle bars. Beware of the 'foot-jamming syndrome'.

Toboggan

It's basically a double seat-grab, but before, turn your bars 90° then grab the seat with both hands and lean back as far as you can, so you're virtually sitting behind the back wheel.

360

Make sure you have a lot of speed and start turning really early. Basically, use your body weight to throw the back end round, spin as quickly as you can, and good luck!!!

Truck driver
A 360 with a barspin thrown in.

Recliner
Take both feet off the pedals and bring them up to the underside of the bars.

Next, let go with your hands, put them behind your head, lean back as far as you can and recline.

Ceran wrap
Big air!! Lift away your left hand and then your left leg. Place your left leg over your left arm and then grab the bars again with your left hand, and do the same on the other side – quickly!!

Heart attack
Firstly, do a Superman but let go with your left hand and grip the seat, then pull yourself up into a handstand over both the bars and seat.

Cordova

Take your feet off the pedals and put them on the bars. Don't let go with your hands. Tense your arms and legs then lean back, arching your back as much as possible and looking up at the sky.

Decade air

This is impossible, so forget it. However, if you're nuts enough, then you need to take your feet off the pedals and spin 360° on the front wheel with the bars around the front of the bike, keeping the frame flying straight. Get your legs over the frame on the way back round and back on to the pedals. Then ride away looking smug...

Maintenance and tech tips

Tools

Before working
on your rig
you'll need a
good set of
tools. Here's a
few of the
necessities:
socket set,
Allen key set,
pump, chain

breaker (don't waste your time with a nail and a hammer), rubber mallet (for those difficult bits), wire cutters, electrical tape, spoke wrenches, puncture repair kit, tyre irons, wd-40, grease and chain lube.

Before working on your bike, give it a really good clean. This will help you see rust spots and cracks easier, plus it's nice to have a fresh bike now and again.

Wheels and tyres

Firstly, check you have no dents in the rims, and no broken spokes (these can damage your tyres).

Check your spokes are tight (simply plucking them and listening to the note will give you some indication). If the spokes feel a little too tricky, then take them to a shop for peace of mind.

Check your wheel nuts are tight. Don't get too carried away tightening or you may ruin the nuts' thread.

Check your tyres for wear or flat spots. A new set is cheap and will make a lot of difference. If your tyres are old then look for dry cracking spots – another sign that it's time for a fresh pair.

Use your pump to sort out your tyre pressure (this detail will be written on the tyre).

Stand above the bike and look down on your wheel and the alignment. If it is out of line then it could be either a bent rim or you might need to change your wheel spacing washers.

Clean your rims, make sure there is no grease on them or your brakes won't work properly. Use a little white spirit and a rag to clean them.

Brakes

Check the wear on your brake pads. If they are worn then replace them.

Check that they line up neatly on the rims when you squeeze the brakes.

Check the cable. Look for kinks or frays. If the ends of the cables are frayed then use the wire cutters to neaten off the ends.

Use electrical tape to keep the cable neat to the frame, but make sure you leave enough slack.

Check your brake lever is tight to the bars.

Oil your brake joints but be careful not to get oil on the brake pads or the rims.

Cranks and chain

Shake your cranks' arms to see if there is any rattle or movement. If there is,

your bearings are probably worn and you may need a replacement.

Check the teeth on your sprocket. If they are worn they could cause your chain to slip, or even break.

Check your chain tension. There needs to be about half an inch play in the chain's vertical movement. If it is too slack or too tight, then loosen off your back wheel and move its position until you're satisfied.

Make sure your chain is well lubed. A dry chain will be noisy and cause wear on your sprocket. Use chain lube, but don't overdo it or you'll turn your chain into a dust magnet.

Seat

Check you are
comfy with
your seat
position and
that your
stem and seat
bolts are tight.

Make sure
your bike is
well oiled and
all your nuts
and bolts are
tight before
you ride.

Tips on lightening your bike

Everyone wants their bike to be a little lighter, so here's a few things to change:

If you don't use your gyro then get rid of it. A properly slacked brake cable will still let you do a barspin.

Stick to two-piece dirt bars. A good pair is by far tough enough.

Tyres all vary in weight – pick the lightest.

Use a good set of 36-spoke rims instead of your 48-spokers.

Change your crank to a three-piece tubular crank.

If you are a dirt jumper you don't need thick, heavy-duty dirt chains. A standard chain will take the pressure and save you some weight.

Get rid of a brake or two.

Use a lightweight seat and a shorter seat stem.

How to build dirt jumps

Get kitted up

Firstly, you need a nice plot of good flat land with good soil (no roots and rocks).

Take with you a couple of shovels, a rake, a wheelbarrow, a couple of gallons of water, and some friends.

Take plenty of food and drinks because this will take a while.

Plan it out

Make sure you leave enough room for a good fast run up and landing, and if you're planning to build more than one set, make sure you plan your whole trail in advance or it could get a bit crowded.

The best place is to find a run up with a little downwards slope to help get your speed up, because you'll want to hit those jumps pretty fast, and as you get better, you'll want to make them bigger and bigger.

If you are building in a wood then don't go cutting up trees. Don't forget that roots can make a good bases for a jump.

Getting started

If you're a beginner then start with a jump between 2 to 3 feet high.

This is enough to get started with because the principle to jumping a 2-footer and a 6-footer is same, so don't feel chicken about it.

A good gap for this size jump is about 6 to 8 feet, so use a stick to measure out this distance between your jump ramp and your landing ramp.

Next, get some dirt together. You can get your dirt from the gap in between your jumps if you want to make your jumps more interesting, but beware that your jump could collapse into the gap.

Make sure your earth is as pure as possible. No sticks or stones should get in the way as they could break your bones and they make packing down the ramps a lot harder. Remember you will always need about twice as much earth as you think.

Start your two piles either side of your gap. The piles need to be about 4 feet wide.

Now you should be ready to start packing down the earth. Bring in your most horizontally-challenged riding friend, and get them to walk up and down the ramp.

Use the flat edge of your shovel to pack the top and the sides. Then add water to help compress the dirt. Don't worry about the shape of the ramp yet, just keep doing this until you have two hard packed mounds.

Shaping the ramp

The take-off ramp needs to have a
perfectly smooth take-off curve with the
lip of the ramp a few degrees off vertical.

Use the sharp edge of the shovel to scrape
down the ramp to create the curve. Make
sure the curve is as smooth and equally
balanced as possible.

As you are carving out the shape, make
sure you keep packing down the top and
sides, so that the jump doesn't crumble.

Don't worry if your take-off looks a little
too steep – it won't be.

Use your bike as a roller to help pack and smooth the curve, and keep packing down the flat top of the ramp to make it really solid.

When you have made the perfect ramp, sprinkle a little water over it to help the earth settle and then leave it.

Your landing ramp doesn't need to have such a steep curve.

Make sure the flat blends smoothly into the descent. It also needs to be twice as long and a little wider to help you down smoothly.

Note that the steeper the landing curve, the faster you will approach the next jump.

Water down this ramp to make it nice and hard.

Don't ride the ramp when it's wet because it will groove and probably collapse.

It's hard to resist but it's better to wait a day or two for the ramps and jumps to settle.

If you decide to ignore this piece of advice...just go for it!

Top Tips

• Get a little extra life out of your brake shoes by turning them around.

• If you get a flat, and need to ride home, but don't have a puncture repair kit, stuff your tyre with grass so it's rideable without ruining your rims.

• If you are a dirt jumper, put a slick tyre on the back and dirt on the front. This gives you both speed and grip.

• If you ride dirt then you probably don't need your back brake. Getting rid of it will lighten up the bike and it won't get in the way.

• If your bars keep slipping try sanding off the paint around the area that the stem camps on, but be careful not to sand off the knurling on your bars.

• When tightening the Allen key bolts on the stem, tighten them in an X pattern.

Websites for BMXers

If you want to check out information on the best places to go BMXing, where to buy BMX rigs and equipment, or to find out about nationwide competitions, the Net is the place to go. Here are just a few UK-based sites.

www.kingofconcrete.com

www.seventies.co.uk

www.backyardjam.com

www.bmxonline.co.uk

www.2670.co.uk

www.byke.com/ukflat

Now you can order other ACCESS ALL AREAS and text-messaging books direct from Michael O'Mara Books Limited.

All at £1.99 each including postage (UK only).

ACCESS ALL AREAS

BRITNEY SPEARS	ISBN 1-85479-790-5
CHRISTINA AGUILERA	ISBN 1-85479-780-8
CRAIG DAVID	ISBN 1-85479-948-7
EMINEM	ISBN 1-85479-793-X
S CLUB 7	ISBN 1-85479-036-3

ACCESS ALL AREAS

SNO	ISBN 1-85479-138-9
HOOPZ	ISBN 1-85479-143-5
SK8	ISBN 1-85479-133-8

TEXT-MESSAGING TITLES

WAN2TLK? ltle bk of txt msgs	ISBN 1-85479-678-X
RUUP4IT? ltle bk of txt d8s	ISBN 1-85479-892-8
LUVTLK: ltle bk of luv txt	ISBN 1-85479-890-1
IH8U: ltle bk of txt abuse	ISBN 1-85479-832-4
URGr8! ltle bk of pwr txt	ISBN 1-85479-817-0

Itle bk of pics & tones   ISBN 1-85479-563-5
WIZTLK! Itle bk of txt spells   ISBN 1-85479-478-7
SEXTLK! Itle bk of sext   ISBN 1-85479-487-6

All Michael O'Mara titles are available by post from:
Bookpost, PO Box 29, Douglas, Isle of Man IM99 1BQ

Credit cards accepted. Please telephone 01624-836000
fax: 01624-837033
Internet http://www.bookpost.co.uk
e-mail: bookshop@enterprise.net

Free postage and packing in the UK. Overseas customers allow
£1 per book (paperbacks) and £3 per book (hardbacks).